GYMNASTICS

by Ruth Mattison

Pioneer Valley Educational Press, Inc.

TABLE OF CONTENTS

AN EXCITING SPORT

Do you like to jump, somersault,
and stand on your head?
Maybe gymnastics is the sport for you.
Gymnastics is an exciting sport
that can make you strong and healthy.

Athletes who are gymnasts must be strong, fit, and agile and have a good sense of balance. To get ready to do gymnastics, gymnasts do a lot of running, jumping, and tumbling.

In gymnastics, there are some events that both boys and girls compete in, and there are some events that are only for boys or that are only for girls.

THE BARS

Female gymnasts need a lot of strength and **flexibility** to do **routines** on the uneven parallel bars. The gymnasts do swings, circles, and handstands while competing on the uneven bars.

Male gymnasts must be very strong
to compete on the high bars.
They swing around the bar,
twist, and change direction.
At the end, they will do flips
or somersaults in the air
before landing on the floor.
This is called a dismount.

Male gymnasts must also be very strong and **coordinated** to perform on the parallel bars. The gymnasts must swing above, between, and beneath the bars using only their hands and arms.

THE VAULT

Both male and female gymnasts compete on the vault. Gymnasts run down a runway, jump onto a springboard, and spring onto the vault.

Next, gymnasts use their hands to push off the vault, leap into the air, and twist and turn before landing on the mat.

Only female gymnasts compete on the balance beam. The beam is 4 inches wide and 4 feet above the floor.

Gymnasts need a good sense of balance and also need to be flexible to do the jumps, somersaults, spins, back flips, and cartwheels they perform on the balance beam.

15

THE STILL RINGS

The still rings are an event only male gymnasts compete in. The still rings require a great deal of upper body strength. A gymnast must do a series of swinging moves while keeping the rings as still as possible. This is very difficult!

The pommel horse is another event for male gymnasts. This event has been around for 600 years. The first pommel horses looked more like real horses.

A gymnast must be both strong and **nimble** to compete on the pommel horse. The gymnast supports his weight on two handles, called pommels, and swings both legs in a circle.

FLOOR EXERCISES

Both female and male gymnasts compete in floor exercises.

Female gymnasts perform a routine to music on floor mats. The routine has somersaults, flips, jumps, and dance moves.

INJURIES

Gymnastics can be a dangerous sport. There is always the danger of falling. Gymnasts can also damage their joints, bones, and muscles.

Warming up and cooling down are important parts of gymnastics that may help prevent injuries. It is also important to have good equipment and good coaching to stay safe.

GLOSSARY

coordinated: to move different parts of the body together easily

flexibility: the ability to bend easily

nimble: able to move quickly

routine: a series of movements that make a performance

INDEX